Book design and layout by Walter Bjorkman

ISBN-13: 978-1511599979
ISBN-10: 1511599979

Blood Medals

Claudia Cortese

Dawn—
to an amazing
teacher & amazing
poet! I hope you
enjoy these
little Lucy
poems! ⚹

XO,
Claudia
Cortese

For Boris, always—

Claudia Cortese's "Lucy" poems are treacherously alive and important. Cortese navigates Lucy's interior world with gorgeous starkness, refusing to be saccharine; rather, Lucy churns with playful viscera and violent intelligence: she is the kind of girl who "demands Santa stitch her a skin of bees, that her screams be not sound but solid: a stinger that stings and stings." These prose poems are raw and fanatically simple, yet every trope is electric-charged, hot to the touch.

—Rusty Morrison

Driven by and into decay, darkness, and rot, Claudia Cortese understands the importance of looking directly into the truth of things, no matter how troubling and terrifying that truth might be. Navigating through the hauntingly sensual language of tumors, shrieking, sores, and knives, *Blood Medals* reveals the sinister underbellies of this world while still managing to glitter with the hope of transcendence. Each poem holds you by the skin on the back of your neck and dares you to look at where your own darkness hides. Cortese's voice is morbidly beautiful, brutally honest, and "brighter than fire and cardinal." *Blood Medals* will leave you haunted and broken and begging for more.

—Meghan Privitello

Table of Contents

Lucy lives in her gauze house,

a little terry cloth tumor. To live here is to be beautiful but very sad.
The girls in Lucy's class tuck their hands under their thighs. They
flock together like grackles. Lucy arranges pebbles in a circle, puts a
G.I. Joe in the middle and lights him on fire. At night, she turns the
mirrors to the walls, belly to tile floor—dreams a matted mange of a
pup loves her best. Lucy knows she's not like the girls. They carry
compacts in their left pockets—powder their chins, glitter their lids: a
little pink goes a long way. If they opened Lucy's box, shared snicker-
doodles and milkshakes, Lucy would say, I love my terry cloth house
more than my mother.

The field curdles

in June heat : Lucy plucks her leg hair with tweezers : floats her
hairless body through those rotting distances : she sees herself :
knobs in her forehead : green-horned girl limps uphill! : a darking
shriek : her dress casing her face—

The birds inside her

are dying. There are blue wings at her window. Why won't you look at me, said the wren to the sparrow. The sickness starts in the trees, then pustules engulf the throat. . . . Lucy tells her sister that ant families burrow beneath them, a small apocalypse with each step— that six-pack rings strangle sea turtles. Lucy braids grassblade and honeysuckle, crowns herself the queen of Edgemont Park. Night falls like a noose, and they leave as the molesters file in. The pomegranate is sweeter than the artichoke, and Lucy loves her sister more than her Cyndi Lauper sweatshirt.

Lucy loves their dead edges,

their lying light. The dim one in the sky's eastern corner has lived a long life. A feral burst of dust, she fought and fucked her way into adulthood, settled into her bed of gold and told the circling moons of her youthful storms—their most numinous moments. Brighter than fire and cardinal, ruby ring pops and maraschinos, the red star beside it has no stories to tell. In other words, Lucy loves her best of all. The spruces in the distance look like a row of pointy caps on trolls' heads, and the Oreos crunching in Lucy's ears are so loud, she fears her mother will hear her mouth.

What Lucy's World Looks Like

Three branches strangled
in telephone wire. The chain
links of a fence.

Not the red swings behind it,
but maple leaves on the slide
rotting under snow.

The oil stain on the wall
with tomato skin stuck to it.
A strip of negatives—

the photo's seared palm.
Black rings, and the raccoon
crawling up the stairs.

Lucy tells the boy to suck

till her arm pockmarks, that if he stops she'll expose what happens at playground's edge. Back home, Lucy decks the tree in Barbie heads, watches snow cut the landscape, all those little white knives. She leaves a hill of Jujubes where her mother's ant traps should be. Lucy loves the carmine glory of her arm, the blood medals of a champion! She calls Milo to her, bites his fur till the roots let go. His yelps shine like sequins, the way snow is sequins, and her arms. Lucy demands Santa stitch her a skin of bees, that her screams be not sound but solid: a stinger that stings and stings.

Lucy sticks a stick

In an anthill, carries it to the other side of the yard. Ant sisters scurry to find their wiry brothers, their mothers with bellies like fat black beads. Lucy scrapes the sandbox, writes tangerine and starblade and dead girls glow prettiest. She cuts a caterpillar. Throws one green half in the grass. Puts the other in her mouth.

When Mrs. Johnstone

says that Edna Pontellier walked into the ocean, let water close above
her because it was her only escape from the Cult of Domesticity, Lucy
sees a group of robed housewives kill a goat then bow to a golden six-
foot toaster oven. She wants to walk into the ocean before 9th period
gym. Her belly fat bounces up and down when she jogs the track.
There's a tornado watch, and the clouds look like cellulose. Lucy hides
behind a spruce while the other girls run laps; she arrives panting and
unflushed to the finish line.

What Lucy's World Smells Like

Tongue-soot, the root
chalk of rot, that egg-
y air that announces
Cleveland. Lucy wishes
for wisteria and walnut
leaf—powdered
babies lined up like calendar
days: wishes for a star, a clover,
air without seeds, oils
of orange and Ohio
June. Lucy once
walked Midland Avenue
and almost nose-orgasmed—
the honeysuckle breeze,
but that's not the point here.
If I say coke's post-drip
bitters, I'll get close.
Also—high school
showers, their pubic mist,
the first spritz of Nasonex,
steroid's chemical singe—

Lucy plays her favorite game

on repeat: tape the news of Jessica lifted from the well. Rewind slowly, watch her return to her hole.

Lucy plays

frog tail plays bandit plays blacken one toe leave the other pinking. She plays find a place safe and unbreathing, only the eye moves. Plays razor plays marbles tossed in creek, name one water-ring Tampon, the other Blood Wart. Lucy plays with friends. Did you think I'd say alone and with weapon, the kind kids fashion—sewing needle taped to safety pin glued to tooth pick pricking Milo tail or sister lobe. What was your favorite place. Where did your shame begin. Perhaps Lucy's the beloved blonde, handlebar glitter, a party's favorite streamer. Curly-cute and her rot imagined which means alive without odor.

Lucy looks in the mirror and sees

a lidless eye. A hole of lye. The herpes sores the nun's slide show glowed before their fourth grade horror. Sees hairless cat. Trash bag a raccoon teethed open, (if I don't eat for one whole week, she bargained, if I stitch my lips—) its Kool-Aid pool ant-stuck and sunning.

Lucy takes three marbles

and sticks them inside her. At night, the slick tip of a pillow grows
between her thighs. She sees a planter man, thick and tall, blond bush
crowning his head. Sees a chained dog bite the air to his left. When
Lucy pees, marbles drop. The gas station's sign buzzes G s st tion.

Lucy wraps salmon

around her fingers, plucks the pink flesh with her teeth. She must
wash each hand seven times. She must throw the empty box of wild
Alaskan salmon in a bag, wrap it in red, blue, and yellow ribbons.
She presses the Reddi-wip nozzle till her mouth fills with sugary
relief. Walking down the sidewalk, Lucy waves hello to no one,
counts how long the light stays green. Reaching 20 seconds means
her mother dies in a plane crash. The sky, with its white pelts, its
glittering lid, is always with her. In her sleep, a man binds her wrists
and tulip trees unpucker their lips in the wind.

Lucy knows words

live in the trees, rain like locusts when she walks through the forest. Leaves unhook the hurt that curdles in her throat, burns behind her lungs. A cricket's wings cry all night, its wiry torso greening her dreams. Lucy dreams the water that splashed on her leg when she flushed the gas station toilet gave her herpes. She dreams elephant's liquid eyes, an ivory hospital bed—the sun a yellow sail lifting her from her body.

Lucy Mad Lib

I hate myself because _____ (proper noun). Each time I look in the _____ (not mirror: what else reflects), I think _____, _____, _____ (expletives). Let me start again. I remember watching _____ (suburban nature image: Note, the pastoral. Note, white flight. Note, mother stands in lamp-glow you see her at the window. Note, dog blood darkens) and feeling _____ (sentimental/noun) and _____ (violent noun because sincerity terrifies). I combed _____'s (girl name) hair, I washed _____'s (girl name) power-pink jeans; we _____ (sexual verb) and _____ (verb of your choosing): don't tell. I tear hair-roots, stick marbles where I pee because _____ (i.e., basement water). The why again: _____ (what I can't forget), I chew my scab, let go the handlebars, b-b gun a bunny, kick the fat boy, write "Bobby sucks big dicks" on his desk, crowbar a pet turtle from its shell, safety pin my thumb-skin because _____ (you know the answer).

28

What the girls named Lucy / What Lucy named the girls

They said, Lucy Fat Face, Ugly, Stupid, Miss Lardy Lard.

Lucy's names—

Empire Girls Glow Wartiest,

Fungus Furring Basement Corner—

Dad's Stash of Sticky Mags.

Must Girls, Jelly-between-the-Toe Girls, Onion Pits

and Missing Eyelid. Lucy says,

You're the toe-throb ingrown. Your factory shrills

fang the air,

your skin the skin

of drums I bang

to break—

Lucy loves her rust-

fucked doll. Pawn shop musk, dust fuzzing its one finger. If Lucy throws her in the dried-out river, no water-plop no sun-blue sheen. Dirt doll in a dirt scar. Lucy can't braid hair with one hand. Does that make her less girl. She smashes the rust face in the grass, says, Don't you love that minty smell. Then tells the doll a story: The world was created by seven robots who wired it to end by fire. The button that ignites the blaze is hidden deep in a mountain and one man knows how to find it. If he gets really really mad he will press it. The world will end in one fiery ball big as Mars' big toe, if Mars were a foot with a really big toe.

Lucy tilts the mirror of the Cover Girl compact and spots

violet folds. A part of her body doesn't exist and then it does. Lucy
bets her mother cut the hole, stitched the flaps back. She bets the
doctors cheered the shearing on, their hand-claps like a mouth wired
open on a treeless hill as lightning nerves the teeth electric.

What Lucy's World Feels Like

      Lawnmower's teethy jangle—
                    too pretty.
Let me start again: drill

      before anesthesia takes hold, nerve burn.
Nail shaved to bone, its
      bloodthrob. Maw

          of mother-smile, incisor
       tine, the bridge
              negotiating two wars,

a red dress, wire
          hanger, the stage
              deer-lit eye-lit gun-lit—

hand's first shatter—

Sonnet

Your face, vein-lit, bone-lit, lit by fear
you are ugly, no one likes you. Smile,
Lucy, shine like a gun, and one day you'll foam
to amber and golden, a frothy
liquid all the fathers love, their sons
waiting for the day they can drink
in a spray of sprinklers, summer glassdrops,
carbamate grass, Ikea chair, an empty
their boys can't see. Lucy, the unlovely,
the tub that is lard, it seems each decade
there's a new victim, same ganglion
of girls that peck and cackle. In my vision,
you and I banshee the branches, shatter to claw
and turn one gold girl to a blubber of caw.

Acknowledgements

Baltimore Review, Summer 2012, "The field curdles" (third place winner in Baltimore Review's literature contest)

Banango Street, Spring 2015, "What Lucy's World Looks Like"

Blackbird, Spring 2013, "Lucy wraps salmon"

Cross Poetry, May 2015, "What the girls named Lucy / What Lucy named the girls"

DIAGRAM, April 2012, "The birds inside her" and "When Mrs. Johnstone"

Meridian, Spring 2012, "Lucy lives in her gauze house" (under the title "Lucy lives in a box")

Rattle, Winter 2011, "Lucy sticks a stick" (under the title "Sarah's mother makes her long dresses of lace")

Phoebe, Fall 2014, "What Lucy's World Feels Like"

Rhino Poetry, Spring 2013, "Lucy tells the boy to suck" (Editor's Prize, third place)

Revolution House, Winter 2013, "Lucy knows words" and "Lucy loves their dead edges"

Winter Tangerine Review, Shedding Skins Feature, April 2015, "Lucy looks in the mirror and sees," "Lucy loves her rust-", "Lucy plays her favorite game" and "Lucy Mad Lib"

Winter Tangerine Review, Issue 5, "Lucy plays," "What Lucy's World Smells Like" and "Sonnet"

Thank you to my family: my mother who encouraged me to become a poet and who has the biggest darn heart of any human ever; my father who bought me *Baby-Sitters Club* books as a girl and Tolstoy novels as an adult: you showed me how to love literature; my twin sister Natalie—our bodies our spirits our stories are twined forever; and my older brother Joe who played me Bikini Kill and showed me John Waters films and taught me weird is not wrong.

Thank you to my sweetie, Boris Tsessarsky, for encouraging me to believe in my work and risk living with crazy literary life. You inspire me daily with your stories and smarts, your love and laughter.

Huge thanks to my dear friends and trusted readers: Grey Vild, Traci Brimhall, Joy Ladin, Rusty Morrison, Brynn Saito, Bekah Sankey, Gillian Cummings, Mike Soto, Liz Martin, Alan Hill, Kem Joy Ukwu, Darin Patterson, Cathy Burns, Nikki Leper, Shauna Leonard, Melanie Wilson, Alex Noussias, Mara Scott, Jen Pattap, Aaron Pattap, Arielle Baer, Duke (Clarkson Fisher III), Christopher Salerno, Staci Schoenfeld, Caleb Kaiser, Jessica Rohrbach, Megan Williams, Shannon Hardwick, Cori Winrock, Meghan Privitello, Trace Peterson, Autumn Linn, Serenity Fisher, Uchechi Kalu Jacobson, and Monica McClure. To anyone I am forgetting—my apologies!

Special thank you to Ocean Vuong and Helen Vitoria for giving my little Lucy such a lovely home.

Claudia Cortese has a forthcoming chapbook, *The Red Essay and Other Histories* (Horse Less Press). Her poems have appeared in *Best New Poets 2011*, *Blackbird*, *Crazyhorse*, *Kenyon Review Online*, and *Sixth Finch*, and her essays and reviews have found homes at *Black Warrior Review*, *Mid-American Review*, and *Iowa Review*, among others. Her first book of poetry has been a finalist for prizes from the Crab Orchard Series in Poetry and Black Lawrence Press. An Ohio Native, Cortese lives in New Jersey and is the poetry editor for *Swarm* (swarmlit.com).

19710562R00025

Made in the USA
Middletown, DE
01 May 2015